PRACTICING STOICISM

A Daily Journal with Meditation Practices, Self-Reflections and Ancient Wisdom from Marcus Aurelius

JASON HEMLOCK

PRACTICING STOICISM:
A Daily Journal with Meditation Practices, Self-Reflections and Ancient Wisdom from Marcus Aurelius
by Jason Hemlock

ISBN: 979-8724526241

CONTENTS

FOREWORD

In order to maximize the value that you receive from this book, I encourage you to check out my first book, *Stoicism: How to Use Stoic Philosophy to Find Inner Peace and Happiness*. All of the daily exercises presented here will be based off of its concepts, so reading it before and/or at the same time will help you get the most out of this one.

Also, as a way of saying thank you for purchasing this book, I'm offering a three-page stoicism cheat sheet for FREE. All you have to do is sign up for my email list, where you will also receive updates and future content from me. The cheat sheet includes quotes from some of my favorite stoics and a short summary of the principles that were discussed in this book, which you can use for future reference.

You can sign up here: bouchardpublishing.com/stoicism.

I also encourage you to join our tight-knit community on Facebook, where you will be able to connect with like-minded people and share your stoic challenges and triumphs to continue your growth. The group name is "Stoicism: The Good Life."

INTRODUCTION

Do you want to feel more content? Appreciate what you have? Be your very best self? Make the most of every moment?

Stoicism can help you achieve all this and more.

In ancient Greece and Rome, philosophers considered the question of what makes a good life. Their philosophies dealt with the universal truths of human existence, and are just as relevant today as they were all those centuries ago.

Neostoicism emerged around twenty years ago. Inspired by the original Hellenistic philosophy, it gives adherents a set of principles and ethics to follow in order to live their very best lives. Stoicism has a strong emphasis on self-discipline and self-improvement, supporting you to achieve your potential and take you further than you may have realized possible.

Stoics accept full responsibility for their thoughts and actions, and work to improve not just their own lives but those of the people around them. It is no coincidence that many successful people have said that they've looked to the Stoics for inspiration.

Stoicism is a practical philosophy, which means that it is not enough to read about it. You have to actually *live* as a Stoic. This can be a daunting prospect, which is why I've created this journal so you can start living a Stoic life and track your progress to see how far you've come, and how far you still need to go.

HOW TO USE THIS JOURNAL

Daily journaling was a very important practice to many of the ancient Greeks and Romans, including Marcus Aurelius, a well-known Stoic. The only Roman emperor who was also a philosopher, he made a point of sitting down every day and reflecting on what he'd learned and how he could be a better man in the future. His notes were never intended for publication, but they were subsequently collated and published as *Meditations,* one of the fundamental texts for anyone wishing to study Stoicism.

This journal contains daily quotes from *Meditations* so you can receive guidance from one of the leading figures in this movement.

Just like Aurelius, you should make time every day to sit down and record your thoughts. Be brutally honest with yourself – this is for your eyes only, so you do not need to hold back. The more honest you are, the more benefit you will get from this process.

This journal follows a simple format. You will start the day by setting your intentions. Decide on what you would like to achieve. These can be small things, like being more patient with your children or spending less time on your phone, or they could be tasks you need to get done for work. It might even be something you intend to do for self-care, like making the time to read a book or meditate. In addition, you will choose a word that you wish to embody that day. You can use the same word more than once or mix it up with a different one every day. Think of things like focus, tolerance, kindness, abundance, determination – words that sum up the attitude you would like to have and will help you on your Stoic journey. Your morning journaling shouldn't take you more than about five minutes.

There is also an exercise for the day. You may decide to do this first thing in the morning or make time to do it later on. Each exercise is designed to embody a specific Stoic principle so that you can really live like a Stoic.

In the evening, you should sit down with your journal and reflect on your day. This will take a little longer than your morning journaling as you look back on what you did well and where you could do better tomorrow.

At the end of sixty days, you will have a record of your Stoic journey so you can look back and see just how far you've come. It can be difficult to see the difference Stoicism is making on a daily basis but when you compare where you are after living Stoically for two months with where you were at the beginning, you'll be pleasantly surprised by how far you've come – and be motivated to keep going.

With space to write the date to personalize your journal, you can come back to this whenever you like to support your Stoicism journey for years to come.

Now that you know how to use this journal and have an understanding of why you should practice Stoicism, you are ready to begin living a Stoic life.

Turn the page and let's get started.

DAY ONE DATE:

____

Morning Journal

What is your profession? Being a good man. But this can only come about through philosophic concepts – concepts of the nature of the Whole, and concepts of the specific constitution of man.

My word for the day is:

____

My top five things to achieve today are:

____

____

____

____

____

Daily Exercise: Practice misfortune

Start your day with a cold shower. Resilience in the face of adversity is a fundamental Stoic principle. If you want to develop the ability to cope with the tough times, actively put yourself in difficult situations so that it is easier to cope when things don't go your way.

Evening Journal

Today I am grateful for:

Did I make decisions in alignment with my best self? Where could I improve?

Was I kind towards the people around me? Where could I have been more considerate?

What temptations did I resist? What vices did I fight?

What was the biggest lesson I learned today?

What can I do better tomorrow?

Any other thoughts:

DAY TWO DATE:

___

Morning Journal

If you remove your judgement of anything that seems painful, you yourself stand quite immune to pain.

My word for today:

___

My top five things to achieve today are:

___

___

___

___

___

Daily Exercise: Turn the obstacle upside down

Make a list of the worst experiences of your life. These might be job losses, relationship breakups, financial difficulties, etc.

Choose one from the list above and write down how you dealt with it. What happened as a consequence?

What else could you have done? Were you aware of these options or did you realise you had alternatives later? How might things have been different if you'd taken a different action?

What opportunities were there within that obstacle? Could you see them at the time? Can you find any more potential opportunities from it?

Now that you can see the opportunities that resulted from that situation, do you still think it was negative, or was it simply something that happened to you and neither inherently good nor bad?

Evening Journal

Today I am grateful for:

____

Did I make decisions in alignment with my best self? Where could I improve?

____

____

____

____

____

Was I kind towards the people around me? Where could I have been more considerate?

____

____

____

____

____

What temptations did I resist? What vices did I fight?

____

____

____

____

____

What was the biggest lesson I learned today?

____

____

____

____

____

What can I do better tomorrow?

____

____

____

____

____

Any other thoughts:

____

____

____

____

____

DAY THREE DATE:

Morning Journal

Is this present thing any reason for my soul to be sick and out of sorts – humbled, craving, shackled, shying? Will you find any good reason for that?

My word for today is:

My top five things to achieve today are:

Practical Exercise: Stay in the moment, for this too will pass

Dance like no one's watching – literally! Choose a song that makes you feel like moving and close your eyes. Let your body start to sway and start dancing in whatever way feels good. Don't worry about how coordinated you are or what you look like. If you can, find somewhere private to dance so you don't feel self-conscious, but if you have children or other family members around, invite them to join you.

Forget about anything except the music playing right now. Give yourself permission to enjoy the moment, let go of any fears, stresses or tension, and just dance. Immerse yourself in the present moment and enjoy it for what it is. A gift to yourself.

Evening Journal

Today I am grateful for:

____

Did I make decisions in alignment with my best self? Where could I improve?

____

____

____

____

____

Was I kind towards the people around me? Where could I have been more considerate?

____

____

____

____

____

What temptations did I resist? What vices did I fight?

____

____

____

____

____

What was the biggest lesson I learned today?

What can I do better tomorrow?

Any other thoughts:

DAY FOUR DATE:

____

Morning Journal

Always have clear in your mind that 'the grass is not greener' elsewhere, and how everything is the same here as on the top of a mountain, or on the sea-shore, or wherever you will.

My word for today is:

____

My top five things to achieve today are:

____

____

____

____

____

Practical Exercise: Take Plato's view

Sit comfortably and just take a moment to focus on your breath. Notice as you inhale and exhale…inhale and exhale…

Now as you inhale, imagine you are breathing in a beautiful, calming white light. And as you exhale, release any negativity or stress you may have been holding on to.

Continue to breathe in that beautiful white light. Feel it filling your body with peaceful energy, making you feel lighter…and lighter…and lighter…

As your body continues to get lighter and lighter, feel yourself starting to float out of your body. You are completely safe as you hover above your body and look down on yourself.

Passively observe yourself sitting there. Notice how you look relaxed and calm and know your body is perfectly safe as you start to float higher and higher.

Now you are outside, hovering above the building your body is in. Look down upon it and see what it looks like from above. Examine the surrounding area – are there gardens? Streets? Cars? Are there people walking around?

Look carefully at the area. Notice all the little details. Think about the people in any buildings you can see going about their business, each of them having their own concerns and worries.

Now rise higher and higher until you are at cloud level. Look down beneath you. See the land stretching out as far as you can see. Notice the curve of the horizon off in the distance.

Feel yourself at peace, knowing you are safe so high in the sky. The world below you seems so small and insignificant, but your journey is not yet done.

You feel yourself going higher again, up, up and out of the atmosphere and into space. You are perfectly safe as you float out towards the moon. Looking back at the earth, it looks like a small ball below you. From this distance, all you can see are the clouds swirling around, the green of the land, the blue of the ocean.

Billions of souls are going about their lives but from this distance, they may as well be dust.

You feel yourself travelling farther and farther away from the earth until you find yourself deep in the heart of the cosmos. All around you are stars, twinkling in a stunning display of natural beauty.

Take a moment to breathe in the wonder around you. Appreciate that everything is as it should be, your life unfolding exactly how it needs to. See the countless stars and know that there are countless more out of sight.

Appreciate that the cosmos is infinite and you are infinitesimal.

When you are ready, take one last deep breath, inhaling the essence of the cosmos, then tell yourself it is time to return to your body.

You find yourself immediately back in your body, sitting where you started. Take a moment to focus on your breath, inhaling and exhaling as you ground yourself fully into yourself.

When you are ready, open your eyes. You might like to journal your experience.

Evening Journal

Today I am grateful for:

Did I make decisions in alignment with my best self? Where could I improve?

Was I kind towards the people around me? Where could I have been more considerate?

What temptations did I resist? What vices did I fight?

What was the biggest lesson I learned today?

What can I do better tomorrow?

Any other thoughts:

DAY FIVE DATE:

____

Morning Journal

Let no one have the chance to accuse you, with any truth, of not being sincere or a good man.

My word for today is:

____

My top five things to achieve today are:

____

____

____

____

____

Practical Exercise – Focus on what you can control

Create a Wheel of Life. Draw a circle and divide it into six segments to represent different areas of your life: family, friends, relationships, career, social life, and spiritual life.

In each segment describe where you are and give it a score out of ten to reflect how satisfied you are with that part of your life.

Now create a second wheel and describe where you would like to be in order to award yourself a ten.

What do you notice? Which areas of your life need attention? Which parts are you happy with and don't want to change?

You cannot control other people's emotions or behaviours, but you can decide to take action to improve your current circumstances and work towards enjoying your best life. This exercise allows you to be objective about where you are and where you want to be.

Evening Journal

Today I am grateful for:

Did I make decisions in alignment with my best self? Where could I improve?

Was I kind towards the people around me? Where could I have been more considerate?

What temptations did I resist? What vices did I fight?

What was the biggest lesson I learned today?

What can I do better tomorrow?

Any other thoughts:

DAY SIX DATE:

____

Morning Journal

What is my directing mind to me? What am I turning it into now, what use am I making of it? Is it drained of intelligence? Is it divorced and broken off from society?

My word for today is:

____

My top five things to achieve today are:

____

____

____

____

____

Practical Exercise - Focus on what you can control with goal setting

Now that you've created your Wheel of Life, it should be obvious which areas of your life need improvement. The next step is to set goals for achieving the kind of life you want. It is important to keep your focus on what you can actively do rather than worrying about results. If, for example, you would like a more fulfilling career, look at what you need to do to get there. Do you need to do any training? Networking? Are there any events you can go to so you can meet people in the industry you want to work in? Or maybe you'd like to set up a business. What steps do you need to take to do this? Maybe you want to improve your advertising, so you can set yourself a goal of doing a post on social media every day or you can say you're going to book yourself on a course to improve your skills.

Make a list of all your goals and the steps you need to take to get to your final destination. Then create a realistic schedule and hold yourself accountable to it.

Evening Journal

Today I am grateful for:

Did I make decisions in alignment with my best self? Where could I improve?

Was I kind towards the people around me? Where could I have been more considerate?

What temptations did I resist? What vices did I fight?

What was the biggest lesson I learned today?

What can I do better tomorrow?

Any other thoughts:

DAY SEVEN DATE:

____

Morning Journal

Calm acceptance of what comes from a cause outside yourself, and justice in all activity of your own causation. In other words, impulse and action fulfilled in that social conduct, which is an expression of your own nature.

My word for today is:

____

My top five things to achieve today are:

____

____

____

____

____

Practical Exercise – Training your mind to accept your fate

Training your mind can be one of the most powerful gifts you can give yourself. The principle of *Amor Fati* is one of the foundations of a Stoic philosophy, and learning to accept things as they are is an effective way to enjoy a more positive mindset.

Look yourself in the mirror and say, "I accept today as it is, not as I would like it to be." Let this be your attitude for today. Whenever you notice yourself sliding into thinking about the future or the past, repeat this mantra to bring your attention back to the present.

You might find it helpful to wear an elastic band around your wrist. Every time your thoughts stray away from the present, ping the band against your wrist so that you experience a mild discomfort. This will help you keep your attention where it needs to be.

Evening Journal

Today I am grateful for:

____

Did I make decisions in alignment with my best self? Where could I improve?

____

____

____

____

____

Was I kind towards the people around me? Where could I have been more considerate?

____

____

____

____

____

What temptations did I resist? What vices did I fight?

____

____

____

____

____

What was the biggest lesson I learned today?

What can I do better tomorrow?

Any other thoughts:

DAY EIGHT DATE:

____

Morning Journal

Joy varies from person to person. My joy is if I keep my directing mind pure, denying no human being or human circumstance, but looking on all things with kindly eyes, giving welcome or use to each as it deserves.

My word for today is:

____

My top five things to achieve today are:

____

____

____

____

____

Practical Exercise – Stoic reflection

Choose a Stoic quote that speaks to you and write your thoughts on what it means and how you can incorporate it into your practises. Do you think this will be easy or difficult for you? What challenges can you anticipate and how can you overcome them?

Evening Journal

Today I am grateful for:

Did I make decisions in alignment with my best self? Where could I improve?

Was I kind towards the people around me? Where could I have been more considerate?

What temptations did I resist? What vices did I fight?

What was the biggest lesson I learned today?

What can I do better tomorrow?

Any other thoughts:

DAY NINE DATE:

____

Morning Journal

In your actions, don't procrastinate. In your conversations, don't confuse. In your thoughts, don't wander. In your soul, don't be passive or aggressive. In your life, don't be all about business.

My word for today is:

____

My top five things to achieve today are:

____

____

____

____

____

Practical Exercise – Water down your vices

The Greeks and Romans always diluted their wine with water. Those who didn't were viewed as having no self-discipline. Romans and Greeks made their wine strong, so if you wanted to enjoy and savour it, you needed to add water so the taste wasn't as strong and you could drink more without worrying about getting drunk.

It's an important metaphor for how you should live as a Stoic. You can have and do anything you want, but in moderation. That way, you don't risk losing your way from a virtuous path by being distracted by your vices.

Make a list of all your vices, bad habits, or things you allow yourself to have but know you 'shouldn't.' Think about what your best self would do – are there any things you do that you know are not in alignment but you make allowances for?

Now think about how you could water them down. If you think you can give them up completely, great, but that's not the purpose of this exercise. You are looking for realistic ways in which you can still enjoy your vices while minimizing their impact. For example, if you like sugar in your tea or coffee, switch to sweetener or half the amount you use. If you spend your evenings binge watching Netflix, limit yourself to a couple episodes of a show and read a good book instead, e.g. *Meditations* by Marcus Aurelius.

Evening Journal

Today I am grateful for:

___

Did I make decisions in alignment with my best self? Where could I improve?

___

___

___

___

___

Was I kind towards the people around me? Where could I have been more considerate?

___

___

___

___

___

What temptations did I resist? What vices did I fight?

___

___

___

___

___

What was the biggest lesson I learned today?

____

What can I do better tomorrow?

Any other thoughts:

DAY TEN DATE:

____

Morning Journal

Dig inside yourself. Inside there is a spring of goodness ready to gush at any moment, if you keep digging.

My word for today is:

____

My top five things to achieve today are:

____

____

____

____

____

Practical Exercise - Loving kindness meditation

As a Stoic, you should aim to act with compassion towards everyone. This loving kindness meditation will help you offer love towards everyone, regardless of how they treat you. The more you recognise that everyone is worthy of love, the easier it becomes to act with kindness in accordance with your best self.

It is best to practice this on a regular basis, which is why you will find it repeated at regular intervals throughout this journal.

Make yourself comfortable with your back supported and close your eyes. Turn your attention to your breath and observe as you inhale and exhale…inhale and exhale…

As you breathe, feel yourself filling with peace and perfect love. With every exhalation, breathe out your stress, fear, and worry, and with every inhalation draw in more peace and love until you feel a deep, fulfilling calmness. Know that the universe loves you. You are worthy of love. You deserve peace and love at all times.

As you feel this beautiful sensation of calm and peace, think of someone you love, your partner, your children, your parents, a close friend. Whoever you think about, send that beautiful peace in their direction. See them being filled with love and harmony until they are as calm and happy as you are in this moment.

Do this again for all your close loved ones.

Now move on to people you are not so close to. Perhaps your colleagues, your neighbours, the person who regularly serves you at your favourite restaurant. Send this love and peace towards them, filling them up with calm, peace, and contentment.

Finally, think about those who have done you wrong, those you do not like, those who have made your life difficult. They too deserve love, so send them the same waves of love and peace, accepting them for who they are and knowing that they are worthy of love because they have taught you valuable lessons and helped you become the person you are today.

When you have finished sending love to everyone who needs it, sit a little longer, feeling this beautiful, peaceful energy.

When you are ready, open your eyes, knowing that this love and peace is always with you.

You may like to journal your experience.

Evening Journal

Today I am grateful for:

____

Did I make decisions in alignment with my best self? Where could I improve?

____

____

____

____

____

Was I kind towards the people around me? Where could I have been more considerate?

____

____

____

____

____

What temptations did I resist? What vices did I fight?

____

____

____

____

____

What was the biggest lesson I learned today?

____

____

____

____

____

What can I do better tomorrow?

____

____

____

____

____

Any other thoughts:

____

____

____

____

____

DAY ELEVEN DATE:

____

Morning Journal

Prepare yourself for the matters that have fallen to your lot, and love these people among whom destiny has cast you – but your love must be genuine.

My word for today is:

____

My top five things to achieve today are:

____

____

____

____

____

Daily Exercise: Practice misfortune

Make your home uncomfortable by adjusting the temperature. If it is cold, turn off your heating so you have to wear extra clothes or wrap up in blankets to stay warm. If it is hot, turn the heat higher so that you cannot cool down. This simple action will make it easier for you to cope if you should ever find yourself in a situation where you don't have access to those luxuries that we all take for granted.

Evening Journal

Today I am grateful for:

____

Did I make decisions in alignment with my best self? Where could I improve?

____

____

____

____

____

Was I kind towards the people around me? Where could I have been more considerate?

____

____

____

____

____

What temptations did I resist? What vices did I fight?

What was the biggest lesson I learned today?

What can I do better tomorrow?

Any other thoughts:

DAY TWELVE DATE:

____

Morning Journal

Do not imagine that, if something is hard for you to achieve, it is therefore impossible for any man; rather, consider anything that is humanly possible and appropriate to lie within your reach too.

My word for today is:

____

My top five things to achieve today are:

____

____

____

____

____

Daily Exercise: Turn the obstacle upside down

Think about a current obstacle in your life. Make a list of all the possible actions available to you, no matter how silly, outrageous, or seemingly impossible. Let your imagination run wild and don't allow yourself to be limited by excuses for why something might not work out. Simply sit and let all the ideas flow until you've run out of inspiration.

Next, make a list of possible outcomes for each one of these actions. Be as honest with these as you can, looking at best- and worst-case scenarios and everything in between. Do not pass judgement on any of these possibilities. Just keep brainstorming until you've dealt with every single idea in as much detail as possible.

Now look at all these outcomes and decide which one best fits your ideal. This is what you need to do to move forward.

Evening Journal

Today I am grateful for:

____

Did I make decisions in alignment with my best self? Where could I improve?

____

____

____

____

____

Was I kind towards the people around me? Where could I have been more considerate?

____

____

____

____

____

What temptations did I resist? What vices did I fight?

____

____

____

____

____

What was the biggest lesson I learned today?

What can I do better tomorrow?

Any other thoughts:

DAY THIRTEEN DATE:

____

Morning Journal

Claim your entitlement to these epithets – good, decent, truthful; in mind clear, cooperative, and independent – and take care then not to swap them for other names: and if you do forfeit these titles, return to them quickly.

My word for today is:

____

My top five things to achieve today are:

____

____

____

____

____

Practical Exercise: Stay in the moment with a mindfulness meditation, for this too will pass

Find somewhere quiet where you won't be interrupted. Have a timer handy. You will need it to keep track of how long you spend on each section and this will also allow you to control how long you meditate. If you only have five minutes, set the timer for one minute. Otherwise, you can set it for up to five minutes depending on how much time you have and how confident you are with meditation. You may also want to eat something small, such as a piece of fruit or chocolate, and have something with a pleasant scent nearby.

Make yourself comfortable. Start your timer and close your eyes. Focus on what you can hear and only what you can hear. What are the obvious noises? What are the quieter noises? Are the noises pleasant or irritating?

When your timer goes off, reset it. With your eyes closed, turn your attention to what you can taste. If you ate before the meditation, how does this feel now? If it's been a while since you've eaten, what does your mouth feel like?

Reset your timer when it goes off. With your eyes closed, concentrate on what you can smell. Are there any strong smells where you are? Can you smell the fragrance of your laundry detergent? Are you wearing perfume? How many smells can you identify?

Reset your timer again when it goes off. With your eyes closed, scan your body to identify what you can feel. What do your clothes feel like against your skin? Are you sitting or lying down? What does the furniture feel like against your body? Be aware of your whole body and your sense of touch.

When your timer goes off, reset it once more. This time, keep your eyes open and gaze around you without judgement. What colours can you see? Is it light or dark? Is there anything moving around you? Can you see something you hadn't noticed?

When your timer goes off, this is the end of the meditation. Take a few minutes to journal your experiences. Which sense was easiest for you to connect to? Which gave you the strongest input? Did you get an emotional response from any of them?

Evening Journal

Today I am grateful for:

Did I make decisions in alignment with my best self? Where could I improve?

Was I kind towards the people around me? Where could I have been more considerate?

What temptations did I resist? What vices did I fight?

What was the biggest lesson I learned today?

_____

_____

_____

_____

_____

What can I do better tomorrow?

_____

_____

_____

_____

_____

Any other thoughts:

_____

_____

_____

_____

_____

DAY FOURTEEN DATE:

Morning Journal

Consider each individual thing you do and ask yourself whether to lose it through death makes death itself any cause to fear.

My word for today is:

My top five things to achieve today are:

Practical Exercise: Memento Mori - Meditation on death

Sit down and make yourself comfortable, ensuring your back is supported.

Take a moment to focus on your breath. Observe it as you inhale and exhale... Inhale and exhale...

And as you inhale, feel that breath filling you with warming energy, helping you relax.

And as you exhale, breathe out any negativity, any stress, any worry.

Continue to inhale that warming energy and exhale any negativity.

Now as you inhale feel yourself sinking down...down...down... Going deep into the earth.

You feel perfectly safe. Nothing can harm you here.

You find yourself standing on the edge of a river. Ahead of you is a small boat, a tall, silent figure dressed in black waiting patiently in the boat for you.

He holds out a hand and beckons you to join him on board.

You realise this is the River Styx, the ferryman, come to take you to the afterlife.

Once you cross this river, you will never be able to return. This is the end of your journey. Once you cross this river, you will be at peace, free from fear and pain.

But once you cross this river, you will never be able to see those you love again.

You imagine how everyone you know will feel when they learn about your passing. What will they say about you? Will they say you lived a good life? Will they say you always tried to do your best?

You think about the decisions you made that you regret. How did you learn from those experiences? How did you use them to do better in the future?

Now you think about the moments when you were at your happiest and felt content. What were you doing? How could you have brought more happiness into your life?

The ferryman beckons to you again, but you shake your head. Now is not your time to travel with him.

He nods, knowing you will return to this place again.

You feel yourself travelling back to your body. Take a moment to appreciate the simple fact you are alive at this time, with a future of possibility ahead of you.

Notice your breath again, feeling gratitude for your life as you inhale and exhale.

And when you are ready, open your eyes.

Journal your experiences.

Evening Journal

Today I am grateful for:

____

Did I make decisions in alignment with my best self? Where could I improve?

____

____

____

____

____

Was I kind towards the people around me? Where could I have been more considerate?

____

____

____

____

____

What temptations did I resist? What vices did I fight?

____

____

____

____

____

What was the biggest lesson I learned today?

___

___

___

___

___

What can I do better tomorrow?

___

___

___

___

___

Any other thoughts:

___

___

___

___

___

DAY FIFTEEN DATE:

____

Morning Journal

'There was a time when I met luck at every turn.' But luck is the good fortune you determine for yourself: and good fortune consists in good inclinations of the soul, good impulses, good actions.

My word for today is:

____

My top five things to achieve today are:

____

____

____

____

____

Practical Exercise – Prepare for the worst

Pick an event you have coming up and list everything that could possibly go wrong or even stop it from happening altogether. Include anything you can think of, no matter how unlikely. For example, nobody could have predicted the pandemic of 2020, but that didn't prevent it from happening, meaning many people had to cancel weddings, holidays, celebrations, etc. As long as something *might* happen, include it on your list. The point of this exercise is to prepare yourself for *every* eventuality.

Once you've completed your list, go back and imagine how it would make you feel if each of the items actually happened. Really immerse yourself in that feeling, as if you're experiencing it right now, so should that event occur, you already know how you'd deal with it.

Finally, for each item, note what you could do to either minimise the likelihood of it occurring or, if it's outside of your control (as most things are), what you can do to minimise its impact. Now, if the worst really does happen, you'll be better equipped to deal with it on every level.

Evening Journal

Today I am grateful for:

___

Did I make decisions in alignment with my best self? Where could I improve?

___

___

___

___

___

Was I kind towards the people around me? Where could I have been more considerate?

___

___

___

___

___

What temptations did I resist? What vices did I fight?

___

___

___

___

___

What was the biggest lesson I learned today?

____

____

____

____

____

What can I do better tomorrow?

____

____

____

____

____

Any other thoughts:

____

____

____

____

____

DAY SIXTEEN DATE:

____

Morning Journal

How have you behaved up to now towards gods, parents, brother, wife, children, teachers, tutors, friends, relations, servants? Has your principle up to now with all of these been 'say no evil, do no evil'?

My word for today is:

____

My top five things to achieve today are:

____

____

____

____

____

____

Practical Exercise – Focus on what you can control with goal setting

It's time to check in on the goals you set for yourself on day 6. How are you doing? Are you meeting your targets or are you slipping?

Evening Journal

Today I am grateful for:

____

Did I make decisions in alignment with my best self? Where could I improve?

____

____

____

____

____

Was I kind towards the people around me? Where could I have been more considerate?

____

____

____

____

____

What temptations did I resist? What vices did I fight?

____

____

____

____

____

What was the biggest lesson I learned today?

What can I do bWhat can I do better tomorrow?

Any other thoughts:

DAY SEVENTEEN DATE:

____

Gladly surrender yourself to Clotho: let her spin your thread into whatever web she wills.

My word for today is:

____

My top five things to achieve today are:

____

____

____

____

____

Practical Exercise – Training your mind to accept your fate

What is more productive: complaining about a problem or finding a solution to the problem?

It's very easy to find a million reasons why you can't do anything to improve your circumstances, but the reality is that there is always something you can do to make life better.

It's only natural to complain when things don't go your way and the occasional vent can be healthy. But when you allow yourself to get caught up in a cycle of complaining, that's energy you could be putting towards making things better. In addition, complaining rarely makes you feel better. It simply reminds you that things aren't as good as you'd like them to be.

Make a commitment that you will not complain about anything today, no matter what. For example, if you get delayed on your way to work, that's okay. Tomorrow you'll leave earlier.

Make a note of how many times you forget and let yourself complain about something.

Evening Journal

Today I am grateful for:

____

Did I make decisions in alignment with my best self? Where could I improve?

____

____

____

____

____

Was I kind towards the people around me? Where could I have been more considerate?

____

____

____

____

____

What temptations did I resist? What vices did I fight?

____

____

____

____

____

What was the biggest lesson I learned today?

What can I do bWhat can I do better tomorrow?

Any other thoughts:

DAY EIGHTEEN DATE:

____

Morning Journal

In every impulse give what is right: in every thought, stick to what is certain.

My word for today is:

____

My top five things to achieve today are:

____

____

____

____

____

____

Practical Exercise - Stoic reflection

Choose a Stoic quote that speaks to you and write your thoughts on what it means and how you can incorporate it into your practises. Do you think this will be easy or difficult for you? What challenges can you anticipate and how can you overcome them?

Evening Journal

Today I am grateful for:

____

Did I make decisions in alignment with my best self? Where could I improve?

____

____

____

____

____

Was I kind towards the people around me? Where could I have been more considerate?

____

____

____

____

____

What temptations did I resist? What vices did I fight?

____

____

____

____

____

What was the biggest lesson I learned today?

What can I do better tomorrow?

Any other thoughts:

DAY NINETEEN DATE:

____

Morning Journal

The best revenge is not to be like your enemy.

My word for today is:

____

My top five things to achieve today are:

____

____

____

____

____

Practical Exercise - Be your best self

Think about an argument or disagreement you've recently been involved in. Journal your motives and actions. Try and be as objective as possible, as if you were discussing someone else. What did you do wrong? What could you have done differently? Why do you think you behaved in the way you did? What other explanations might there be for your behaviour? How would a Stoic approach have looked?

Next, look at the motives and actions of the other person. What are the possible explanations for why they did what they did? What might be a factor for them that you are unaware of? What might be going on in their life that impacted their reactions to you?

When you are finished, choose the kindest explanation you can come with for the other party's behaviour and the harshest explanation for your own.

Write them down here:

____

____

____

____

____

____

____

____

____

____

How does this change your understanding of the situation? What will you do differently when something similar occurs in the future?

In the future I will:

____

____

____

____

____

____

____

____

Evening Journal

Today I am grateful for:

Did I make decisions in alignment with my best self? Where could I improve?

Was I kind towards the people around me? Where could I have been more considerate?

What temptations did I resist? What vices did I fight?

What was the biggest lesson I learned today?

What can I do better tomorrow?

Any other thoughts:

DAY TWENTY DATE:

___

Morning Journal

When circumstances for you lead to some kind of distress, quickly return to yourself. Do not stay out of rhythm for longer than you must: you will master the harmony more by constantly going back to it.

My word for today is:

___

My top five things to achieve today are:

___

___

___

___

___

Practical Exercise - Loving kindness meditation

Make yourself comfortable with your back supported and close your eyes. Turn your attention to your breath and observe as you inhale and exhale…inhale and exhale…

And as you breathe, feel yourself filling with peace and perfect love. With every exhalation, breathe out your stress, fear, and worry, and with every inhalation draw in more peace and love until you feel a deep, fulfilling calmness. Know that the universe loves you. You are worthy of love. You deserve peace and love at all times.

As you feel this beautiful sensation of calm and peace, think of someone you love, your partner, your children, your parents, a close friend. Whoever you think about, send that beautiful peace in their direction. See them being filled with love and harmony until they are as calm and happy as you are in this moment.

Do this again for all your close loved ones.

Now move on to people to whom you are not so close. Perhaps your colleagues, your neighbours, the person who regularly serves you at your favourite restaurant. Send this love and peace towards them, filling them up with calm, peace, and contentment.

Finally, think about those who have done you wrong, those you do not like, those who have made your life difficult. They, too, deserve love, so send them the same waves of love and peace, accepting them for who they are and knowing that they are worthy of love because they have taught you valuable lessons and helped you become the person you are today.

When you have finished sending love to everyone who needs it, sit a little longer, feeling this beautiful, peaceful energy.

When you are ready, open your eyes, knowing that this love and peace is always with you.

Evening Journal

Today I am grateful for:

___

Did I make decisions in alignment with my best self? Where could I improve?

___

___

___

___

___

Was I kind towards the people around me? Where could I have been more considerate?

___

___

___

___

___

What temptations did I resist? What vices did I fight?

___

___

___

___

___

What was the biggest lesson I learned today?

What can I do better tomorrow?

Any other thoughts:

DAY TWENTY-ONE DATE:

____

Morning Journal

The art of living is more like wrestling than dancing, in that it stands ready for what comes and is not thrown by the unforeseen.

My word for today is:

____

My top five things to achieve today are:

____

____

____

____

____

Daily Exercise: Practise misfortune

Limit the amount of money you have to spend. If you go out regularly, it can be easy to spend without thinking. If you have a social event coming up, take a small amount of cash with you, less than you would usually spend, and once it's gone, don't spend any more.

Take this exercise a step further and limit how much you will spend over a month. Sit down and budget how much you absolutely have to spend on essential bills and then drastically limit the amount you will spend from what's left, e.g., by 75%. Put the money you aren't allowing yourself to spend in a savings account and adjust your lifestyle accordingly.

Evening Journal

Today I am grateful for:

____

Did I make decisions in alignment with my best self? Where could I improve?

____

____

____

____

____

Was I kind towards the people around me? Where could I have been more considerate?

What temptations did I resist? What vices did I fight?

What was the biggest lesson I learned today?

What can I do better tomorrow?

Any other thoughts:

DAY TWENTY-TWO DATE:

____

Morning Journal

Remember how long you have been putting this off, how many times you have been given a period of grace by the gods and not used it. It is high time now for you to understand the universe of which you are a part, and the governor of that universe of whom you constitute an emanation: and that there is a limit circumscribed to your time – if you do not use it to clear away your clouds, it will be gone, and you will be gone, and the opportunity will not return.

My word for today is:

____

My top five things to achieve today are:

____

____

____

____

____

Daily Exercise: Turn the obstacle upside down

If there is something you would like to do but haven't been able to for whatever reason, make a list of everything that is stopping you or might stop you.

Are those obstacles insurmountable?

Decide on something you would like to achieve. List out all the obstacles you might face.

Now list all the actions you can take to turn these obstacles and use them to your advantage.

What is the first step you need to take towards your goal? Make a commitment to yourself that you will do it today.

Evening Journal

Today I am grateful for:

___

Did I make decisions in alignment with my best self? Where could I improve?

___

___

___

___

___

Was I kind towards the people around me? Where could I have been more considerate?

___

___

___

___

___

What temptations did I resist? What vices did I fight?

___

___

___

___

___

What was the biggest lesson I learned today?

What can I do better tomorrow?

Any other thoughts:

DAY TWENTY-THREE DATE:

___

Morning Journal

Every hour of the day give vigorous attention to the performance of the task in hand with precise analysis, with unaffected dignity, with human sympathy, with dispassionate justice – and to vacating your mind from all its other thoughts.

My word for today is:

___

My top five things to achieve today are:

___

___

___

___

___

Practical Exercise: Stay in the moment, for this too will pass

Decide that you are going to find six new things about your environment today. Actively look for things you haven't noticed before or pay attention to how things have subtly changed since yesterday. Not only will this help you be more mindful, it also demonstrates very obviously how nothing ever stays the same.

Evening Journal

Today I am grateful for:

____

Did I make decisions in alignment with my best self? Where could I improve?

____

____

____

____

____

Was I kind towards the people around me? Where could I have been more considerate?

____

____

____

____

____

What temptations did I resist? What vices did I fight?

____

____

____

____

____

What was the biggest lesson I learned today?

____

____

____

____

____

What can I do better tomorrow?

____

____

____

____

____

Any other thoughts:

____

____

____

____

____

DAY TWENTY-FOUR DATE:

____

Morning Journal

Imagine you are now dead, or had not lved before this moment. Now view the rest of your life as a bonus, and live it as nature directs.

My word for today is:

____

My top five things to achieve today are:

____

____

____

____

____

Practical Exercise – Memento Mori. Plan your funeral

It is always a good idea to plan your own funeral. It's a surprisingly enjoyable experience, but what makes it important is that when you have specific plans for after you're gone, it makes a difficult time a little easier for your loved ones because they don't have to worry about what to organize. Knowing what you want at your funeral is a comfort to those who you leave behind and gives them one final reminder of the kind of person you were.

An important aspect of this process is writing your eulogy. This is the celebration of your life and who you were. Be honest. You don't have to be positive – this is for your own personal use. What will your friends and family say about you? Did you make time for the ones you love? Were you kind to the people around you? Did you always do your best to live your life or could you have done more to be a better person?

Evening Journal

Today I am grateful for:

___

Did I make decisions in alignment with my best self? Where could I improve?

___

___

___

___

___

Was I kind towards the people around me? Where could I have been more considerate?

___

___

___

___

___

What temptations did I resist? What vices did I fight?

___

___

___

___

___

What was the biggest lesson I learned today?

____

____

____

____

____

What can I do better tomorrow?

____

____

____

____

____

Any other thoughts:

____

____

____

____

____

DAY TWENTY-FIVE DATE:

Morning Journal

All that exists will soon change. Either it will be turned into vapour, if all matter is a unity, or it will be scattered in atoms.

My word for today is:

___

My top five things to achieve today are:

___

___

___

___

___

Practical Exercise - Prepare for the worst with visualization

This can be a very emotional exercise, so when you do it, choose a time and place where you won't be disturbed so you can fully immerse yourself in the moment without feeling like you have to self-censor for the sake of those around you.

Choose one of the worst things you could imagine happening to you. It might be losing a loved one; it could be experiencing a life-changing accident; perhaps you want to think about becoming homeless following a redundancy. Pick something that is your absolute worst nightmare, the one thing you really *don't* want to see come true.

Sit yourself comfortably, making sure your back is supported, so you can meditate without being distracted by your body needing to fidget. Close your eyes and imagine someone telling you the news you didn't want to hear. Picture their face, the sadness in their eyes as they tell you what happened and how sorry they are for you. Allow yourself to be flooded with emotion as you feel denial it could be possible, anger that it's happened, sadness that things will never be the same again. If you need to cry, cry.

Don't think about what to do next. This is not the time to come up with contingency plans. Instead, immerse yourself completely in the feelings of the moment. Know that there was absolutely nothing you could have done to change this outcome, so all you can do is accept that this is how it is and adjust your reality accordingly.

This too will pass. No matter how badly you feel in the moment, this moment is not forever.

Evening Journal

Today I am grateful for:

____

Did I make decisions in alignment with my best self? Where could I improve?

____

____

____

____

____

Was I kind towards the people around me? Where could I have been more considerate?

____

____

____

____

____

What temptations did I resist? What vices did I fight?

____

____

____

____

____

What was the biggest lesson I learned today?

What can I do better tomorrow?

Any other thoughts:

DAY TWENTY-SIX DATE:

____

Morning Journal

Up, down, round and round are the motions of the elements, but the movement of active virtue follows none of these: it is something more divine, and it journeys on to success along a path hard to understand.

My word for today is:

____

My top five things to achieve today are:

____

____

____

____

____

Practical Exercise – Focus on what you can control with goal setting

It's time to check in on the goals you set for yourself on day 6. How are you doing? Are you meeting your targets or are you slipping?

Evening Journal

Today I am grateful for:

Did I make decisions in alignment with my best self? Where could I improve?

Was I kind towards the people around me? Where could I have been more considerate?

What temptations did I resist? What vices did I fight?

What was the biggest lesson I learned today?

____

____

____

____

____

What can I do better tomorrow?

____

____

____

____

____

Any other thoughts:

____

____

____

____

____

DAY TWENTY-SEVEN DATE:

____

Morning Journal

Sober up, recall yourself, shake off sleep once more: realize they were mere dreams that troubled you, and now that you are awake again, look on these things as you would have looked on a dream.

My word for today is:

____

My top five things to achieve today are:

____

____

____

____

____

Practical Exercise: Prepare for the worst by talking to your future self

It is a good idea to open up a regular dialogue with your future self. This will help you put into perspective anything negative that comes your way. It's easy to let little things get under your skin, such as when the printer jams or someone lets a door close in your face instead of holding it open for you. But in the grand scheme of things, how much did that really matter? Printers can be fixed. You can open doors for yourself.

There is very little that can have a major negative impact on your future if you take a moment to breathe and put events into context. Even the biggest setbacks life can throw your way lose their hold over you given enough time. That nasty breakup probably won't be haunting you five years from now when you're happily married to the love of your life. That embarrassing foot-in-mouth moment when you said something stupid in an interview for your dream job won't be important when you're running your own company a few years down the line.

Make a commitment that if anything negative happens to you today, before you react you will take a moment to ask yourself: "How will I be feeling about this event in ten years' time?"

If you still find yourself upset, imagine yourself sitting down with yourself 10 years from now. What advice would they give you? Would you be telling yourself not to worry, that everything's going to be all right, it'll all work out in the end?

Journal your experiences.

____

____

____

____

Evening Journal

Today I am grateful for:

Did I make decisions in alignment with my best self? Where could I improve?

Was I kind towards the people around me? Where could I have been more considerate?

What temptations did I resist? What vices did I fight?

What was the biggest lesson I learned today?

____

____

____

____

____

What can I do better tomorrow?

____

____

____

____

____

Any other thoughts:

____

____

____

____

____

DAY TWENTY-EIGHT DATE:

____

Morning Journal

Regret is a censure of yourself for missing something beneficial. The good must be something beneficial, and of concern to the wholly good person. No wholly good person would regret missing a pleasure. Therefore, pleasure is neither beneficial nor a good.

My word for today is:

____

My top five things to achieve today are:

____

____

____

____

____

Practical Exercise – Stoic reflection

Choose a Stoic quote that speaks to you and write your thoughts on what it means and how you can incorporate it into your practises. Do you think this will be easy or difficult for you? What challenges can you anticipate and how can you overcome them?

Evening Journal

Today I am grateful for:

____

Did I make decisions in alignment with my best self? Where could I improve?

____

____

____

____

____

Was I kind towards the people around me? Where could I have been more considerate?

____

____

____

____

____

What temptations did I resist? What vices did I fight?

____

____

____

____

____

What was the biggest lesson I learned today?

What can I do better tomorrow?

Any other thoughts:

DAY TWENTY-NINE DATE:

____

Morning Journal

Do you not see how the working craftsman, while deferring to the layman up to a point, nevertheless sticks to the principle of his craft and will not bear to desert it? Is it not strange, then, that the architect and the doctor will show greater respect for the guiding principle of their craft than man will for his own guiding principle, which he has in common with the gods?

My word for today is:

____

My top five things to achieve today are:

____

____

____

____

____

Practical Exercise – Be your best self

Write a description of someone you know whom you admire and look up to. Why do you feel that way about them? What do they do that makes them worthy of your respect? What is it about their behaviour you would like to emulate?

Now detail what your best self looks like. Think about who you are and who you realistically have the potential to be rather than including qualities you feel 'ought' to be there. Are you successful? What does that success look like? Are you wealthy or content with just having enough to pay the bills? How do you treat other people? What would your life be like if you were always this best version of yourself?

Now think about a situation recently that you found difficult to deal with. How would your best self have reacted? How might things have been different if your best self was in that situation?

Evening Journal

Today I am grateful for:

____

Did I make decisions in alignment with my best self? Where could I improve?

____

____

____

____

____

Was I kind towards the people around me? Where could I have been more considerate?

____

____

____

____

____

What temptations did I resist? What vices did I fight?

____

____

____

____

____

What was the biggest lesson I learned today?

What can I do better tomorrow?

Any other thoughts:

DAY THIRTY DATE:

____

Morning Journal

Have I done something for the common good? Then I too have benefited.

My word for today is:

____

My top five things to achieve today are:

____

____

____

____

____

Practical Exercise – Loving kindness meditation

Make yourself comfortable with your back supported and close your eyes. Turn your attention to your breath and observe as you inhale and exhale…inhale and exhale…

And as you breathe, feel yourself filling with peace and perfect love. With every exhalation, breathe out your stress, fear, and worry, and with every inhalation draw in more peace and love until you feel a deep, fulfilling calmness. Know that the universe loves you. You are worthy of love. You deserve peace and love at all times.

As you feel this beautiful sensation of calm and peace, think of someone you love, your partner, your children, your parents, a close friend. Whoever you think about, send that beautiful peace in their direction. See them being filled with love and harmony until they are as calm and happy as you are in this moment.

Do this again for all your close loved ones.

Now move on to people to whom you are not so close. Perhaps your colleagues, your neighbours, the person who regularly serves you at your favourite restaurant. Send this love and peace towards them, filling them up with calm, peace, and contentment.

Finally, think about those who have done you wrong, those you do not like, those who have made your life difficult. They, too, deserve love, so send them the same waves of love and peace, accepting them for who they are and knowing that they are worthy of love because they have taught you valuable lessons and helped you become the person you are today.

When you have finished sending love to everyone who needs it, sit a little longer, feeling this beautiful, peaceful energy.

When you are ready, open your eyes, knowing that this love and peace is always with you.

You may like to journal your experience.

Evening Journal

Today I am grateful for:

____

Did I make decisions in alignment with my best self? Where could I improve?

____

____

____

____

____

Was I kind towards the people around me? Where could I have been more considerate?

____

____

____

____

____

What temptations did I resist? What vices did I fight?

____

____

____

____

____

What was the biggest lesson I learned today?

____

____

____

____

____

What can I do better tomorrow?

____

____

____

____

____

Any other thoughts:

____

____

____

____

____

DAY THIRTY-ONE DATE:

____

Morning Journal

A bitter cucumber? Throw it away. Brambles on the path? Go round them. That is all you need, without going on to ask 'So why are these things in the world anyway?'

My word for today is:

____

My top five things to achieve today are:

____

____

____

____

____

Daily Exercise: Practise misfortune

For the next week, eat a minimalist diet. Choose a limited number of ingredients or foodstuffs, e.g., rice and beans, bread and cheeses, noodles, etc., and eat nothing but those items. While you do not want to eat such a restricted diet for a prolonged period, consuming only the bare minimum for a short while will demonstrate that it is possible to survive on very little if you have to.

Evening Journal

Today I am grateful for:

____

Did I make decisions in alignment with my best self? Where could I improve?

____

____

____

____

____

Was I kind towards the people around me? Where could I have been more considerate?

____

____

____

____

____

What temptations did I resist? What vices did I fight?

____

____

____

____

____

What was the biggest lesson I learned today?

____

____

____

____

____

What can I do better tomorrow?

____

____

____

____

____

Any other thoughts:

____

____

____

____

____

DAY THIRTY-TWO DATE:

____

Morning Journal

Let any external thing that so wishes happen to those parts of me that can be affected by its happening – and they, if they wish, can complain. I myself am not yet harmed, unless I judge this occurrence something bad: and I can refuse to do so.

My word for today is:

____

My top five things to achieve today are:

____

____

____

____

____

Daily Exercise: Turn the obstacle upside down

Go back to the list of difficult times in your life you made on day two. Choose another one and write down how you dealt with it. What happened as a consequence?

____

____

____

____

____

What else could you have done? Were you aware of these options or did you realise you had alternatives later? How might things have been different if you'd taken a different action?

____

____

____

____

____

What opportunities were there within that obstacle? Could you see them at the time? Can you find any more potential opportunities from it?

____

____

____

____

____

Now that you can see the opportunities that came from that situation, do you still think it was negative or was it simply something that happened to you and neither inherently good nor bad?

____

____

____

____

____

Evening Journal

Today I am grateful for:

____

Did I make decisions in alignment with my best self? Where could I improve?

____

____

____

____

____

Was I kind towards the people around me? Where could I have been more considerate?

____

____

____

____

____

What temptations did I resist? What vices did I fight?

____

____

____

____

____

What was the biggest lesson I learned today?

What can I do better tomorrow?

Any other thoughts:

DAY THIRTY-THREE DATE:

____

Morning Journal

Do not let the future trouble you. You will come to it (if that is what you must) possessed of the same reason that you apply now to the present.

My word for today is:

____

My top five things to achieve today are:

____

____

____

____

____

Practical Exercise: Stay in the moment, for this too will pass

Choose something you do every day, something mundane like drinking that first cup of coffee or cleaning. Slow it right down and pay attention to every single aspect of it. Use all your senses to observe that particular task. What can you see while you're doing it? What do you smell? What can you taste? What do you hear? What can you feel against your skin? In your hands?

Journal how this exercise made you feel.

Evening Journal

Today I am grateful for:

___

Did I make decisions in alignment with my best self? Where could I improve?

___

___

___

___

___

Was I kind towards the people around me? Where could I have been more considerate?

___

___

___

___

___

What temptations did I resist? What vices did I fight?

___

___

___

___

___

What was the biggest lesson I learned today?

What can I do better tomorrow?

Any other thoughts:

DAY THIRTY-FOUR DATE:

Morning Journal

Take a view from above – look at the thousands of flocks and herds, the thousands of human ceremonies, every sort of voyage in storm or calm, the range of creation, combination, and extinction. Consider too the lives once lived by others long before you, the lives that will be lived after you, the lives lived now among foreign tribes; and how many have never even heard your name, how many will very soon forget it, how many may praise you now but quickly turn to blame. Reflect that neither memory nor fame, nor anything else at all, has any importance worth thinking of.

My word for today is:

My top five things to achieve today are:

Practical Exercise: Take Plato's view

Now is a good time to do the Plato's view meditation again. Sit comfortably and just take a moment to focus on your breath. Notice as you inhale and exhale…inhale and exhale…

Now as you inhale, imagine you are breathing in a beautiful, calming white light. And as you exhale, release any negativity or stress you may have been holding on to.

Continue to breathe in that beautiful white light. Feel it filling your body with peaceful energy, making you feel lighter…and lighter…and lighter…

And as your body continues to get lighter and lighter, feel yourself starting to float out of your body. You are completely safe as you hover above your body and look down on yourself.

Passively observe yourself sitting there. Notice how you look relaxed and calm and know your body is perfectly safe as you start to float higher and higher.

Now you are outside, hovering above the building your body is in. Look down upon it and see what it looks like from above. Examine the surrounding area – are there gardens? Streets? Cars? Are there people walking around?

Look carefully at the area. Notice all the little details. Think about the people in any buildings you can see going about their business, each of them having their own concerns and worries.

Now rise higher and higher until you are at cloud level. Look down beneath you. See the land stretching out as far as you can see. Notice the curve of the horizon off in the distance.

Feel yourself at peace, knowing you are safe so high in the sky. The world below you seems so small and insignificant, but your journey is not yet done.

You feel yourself going higher again, up, up and out of the atmosphere and into space. You are perfectly safe as you float out towards the moon. Looking back at the earth, it looks like a small ball below you. From this distance, all you can see are the clouds swirling around, the green of the land, the blue of the ocean.

Billions of souls are going about their lives but from this distance, they may as well be dust.

You feel yourself travelling farther and farther away from the earth until you find yourself deep in the heart of the cosmos. All around you are stars, twinkling in a stunning display of natural beauty.

Take a moment to breathe in the wonder around you. Appreciate that everything is as it should be, your life unfolding exactly how it needs to. See the countless stars and know that there are countless more out of sight.

Appreciate that the cosmos is infinite and you are infinitesimal.

When you are ready, take one last deep breath, inhaling the essence of the cosmos, then tell yourself it is time to return to your body.

You find yourself immediately back in your body, sitting where you started. Take a moment to focus on your breath, inhaling and exhaling as you ground yourself fully into yourself.

When you are ready, open your eyes. You might like to journal your experience.

Evening Journal

Today I am grateful for:

___

Did I make decisions in alignment with my best self? Where could I improve?

___

___

___

___

___

Was I kind towards the people around me? Where could I have been more considerate?

___

___

___

___

___

What temptations did I resist? What vices did I fight?

___

___

___

___

___

What was the biggest lesson I learned today?

____

____

____

____

____

What can I do better tomorrow?

____

____

____

____

____

Any other thoughts:

____

____

____

____

____

DAY THIRTY-FIVE DATE:

____

Morning Journal

Try out too how the life of the good man goes for you.

My word for today is:

____

My top five things to achieve today are:

____

____

____

____

____

Practical Exercise – Focus on what you can control

Revisit the Wheel of Life you created on day 5. How would you change the Wheel reflecting where you currently are? Have you made any progress towards where you would like to be? Where can you make more effort to improve?

Evening Journal

Today I am grateful for:

Did I make decisions in alignment with my best self? Where could I improve?

Was I kind towards the people around me? Where could I have been more considerate?

What temptations did I resist? What vices did I fight?

What was the biggest lesson I learned today?

What can I do better tomorrow?

Any other thoughts:

DAY THIRTY-SIX DATE:

Morning Journal

No, you do not have thousands of years to live. Urgency is on you. While you live, while you can, become good.

My word for today is:

My top five things to achieve today are:

Practical Exercise – Focus on what you can control with goal setting

It's time to check in on the goals you set for yourself on day 6. How are you doing? Are you meeting your targets or are you slipping?

Evening Journal

Today I am grateful for:

___

Did I make decisions in alignment with my best self? Where could I improve?

___

___

___

___

___

Was I kind towards the people around me? Where could I have been more considerate?

___

___

___

___

___

What temptations did I resist? What vices did I fight?

___

___

___

___

___

What was the biggest lesson I learned today?

____

____

____

____

____

What can I do better tomorrow?

____

____

____

____

____

Any other thoughts:

____

____

____

____

____

DAY THIRTY-SEVEN DATE:

____

Morning Journal

Love only what falls your way and is fated for you. What could suit you more than that?

My word for today is:

____

My top five things to achieve today are:

____

____

____

____

____

Practical Exercise - Training your mind to accept your fate

It is time to return to the exercise you did on day 7.

Look yourself in the mirror and say, "I accept today as it is, not as I would like it to be." Let this be your attitude for today. Whenever you notice yourself sliding into thinking about the future or the past, repeat this mantra to bring your attention back to the present.

You might find it helpful to wear an elastic band around your wrist. Every time your thoughts stray away from the present, ping the band against your wrist so that you experience a mild discomfort. This will help you keep your attention where it needs to be.

Evening Journal

Today I am grateful for:

Did I make decisions in alignment with my best self? Where could I improve?

Was I kind towards the people around me? Where could I have been more considerate?

What temptations did I resist? What vices did I fight?

What was the biggest lesson I learned today?

____

____

____

____

____

What can I do better tomorrow?

____

____

____

____

____

Any other thoughts:

____

____

____

____

____

DAY THIRTY-EIGHT DATE:

____

Morning Journal

Change: nothing inherently bad in the process, nothing inherently good in the result.

My word for today is:

____

My top five things to achieve today are:

____

____

____

____

____

Practical Exercise - Stoic reflection

Choose a Stoic quote that speaks to you and write your thoughts on what it means and how you can incorporate it into your practises. Do you think this will be easy or difficult for you? What challenges can you anticipate and how can you overcome them?

Evening Journal

Today I am grateful for:

____

Did I make decisions in alignment with my best self? Where could I improve?

____

____

____

____

____

Was I kind towards the people around me? Where could I have been more considerate?

____

____

____

____

____

What temptations did I resist? What vices did I fight?

____

____

____

____

____

What was the biggest lesson I learned today?

What can I do better tomorrow?

Any other thoughts:

DAY THIRTY-NINE DATE:

____

Morning Journal

Disgraceful if, in this life where your body does not fail, your soul should fail you first.

My word for today is:

____

My top five things to achieve today are:

____

____

____

____

____

Practical Exercise – Water down your vices

Look back at the list of vices you made on day 9. How have you been diluting them? Have you allowed yourself to slip back into bad habits? What improvements could you make?

Evening Journal

Today I am grateful for:

____

Did I make decisions in alignment with my best self? Where could I improve?

____

____

____

____

____

Was I kind towards the people around me? Where could I have been more considerate?

____

____

____

____

____

What temptations did I resist? What vices did I fight?

____

____

____

____

____

What was the biggest lesson I learned today?

What can I do better tomorrow?

Any other thoughts:

DAY FORTY DATE:

____

Morning Journal

What benefits one person benefits other people too.

My word for today is:

____

My top five things to achieve today are:

____

____

____

____

____

Practical Exercise – Loving kindness meditation

Make yourself comfortable with your back supported and close your eyes. Turn your attention to your breath and observe as you inhale and exhale…inhale and exhale…

And as you breathe, feel yourself filling with peace and perfect love. With every exhalation, breathe out your stress, fear, and worry, and with every inhalation draw in more peace and love until you feel a deep, fulfilling calmness. Know that the universe loves you. You are worthy of love. You deserve peace and love at all times.

As you feel this beautiful sensation of calm and peace, think of someone you love, your partner, your children, your parents, a close friend. Whoever you think about, send that beautiful peace in their direction. See them being filled with love and harmony until they are as calm and happy as you are in this moment.

Do this again for all your close loved ones.

Now move on to people to whom you are not so close. Perhaps your colleagues, your neighbours, the person who regularly serves you at your favourite restaurant. Send this love and peace towards them, filling them up with calm, peace, and contentment.

Finally, think about those who have done you wrong, those you do not like, those who have made your life difficult. They, too, deserve love, so send them the same waves of love and peace, accepting them for who they are and knowing that they are worthy of love because they have taught you valuable lessons and helped you become the person you are today.

When you have finished sending love to everyone who needs it, sit a little longer, feeling this beautiful, peaceful energy.

When you are ready, open your eyes, knowing that this love and peace is always with you.

You may like to journal your experience.

Evening Journal

Today I am grateful for:

____

Did I make decisions in alignment with my best self? Where could I improve?

____

____

____

____

____

Was I kind towards the people around me? Where could I have been more considerate?

____

____

____

____

____

What temptations did I resist? What vices did I fight?

____

____

____

____

____

What was the biggest lesson I learned today?

What can I do better tomorrow?

Any other thoughts:

DAY FORTY-ONE DATE:

____

Morning Journal

And what harm can you suffer, if you yourself at this present moment are acting in kind with your own nature and accepting what suits the present purpose of universal nature – a man at full stretch for the achievement, this way or that, of the common good?

My word for today is:

____

My top five things to achieve today are:

____

____

____

____

____

Daily Exercise: Practise misfortune

No matter how bad life gets, there are always others who are worse off. Find a local charity and sign up as a volunteer. This is an exercise in experiencing how hard others have it, so look for something that will push you outside of your comfort zone rather than playing to your strengths. While you may well discover you enjoy volunteering, the purpose of this exercise is not for you to do something you love but to expose you to difficulties. Possibilities include volunteering at a soup kitchen or food bank, cleaning out the dirty bedding at an animal shelter, going litter picking, and many more.

Evening Journal

Today I am grateful for:

____

Did I make decisions in alignment with my best self? Where could I improve?

____

____

____

____

____

Was I kind towards the people around me? Where could I have been more considerate?

____

____

____

____

____

What temptations did I resist? What vices did I fight?

____

____

____

____

____

What was the biggest lesson I learned today?

What can I do better tomorrow?

Any other thoughts:

DAY FORTY-TWO DATE:

____

Morning Journal

Things of themselves cannot touch the soul at all. They have no entry to the soul, and cannot turn or move it. The soul alone turns and moves itself, making all externals presented to it cohere with the judgements it thinks worthy of itself.

My word for today is:

____

My top five things to achieve today are:

____

____

____

____

____

Daily Exercise: Turn the obstacle upside down

Think about a current obstacle in your life. Make a list of all the possible actions available to you, no matter how silly, outrageous, or seemingly impossible. Let your imagination run wild and don't allow yourself to be limited by excuses for why something might not work out. Simply sit and let all the ideas flow until you've run out of inspiration.

Next, make a list of possible outcomes for each one of these actions. Be as honest with these as you can, looking at best- and worst-case scenarios and everything in between. Do not pass judgement on any of these possibilities. Just keep brainstorming until you've dealt with every single idea in as much detail as possible.

Now look at all these outcomes and decide which one best fits your ideal. This is what you need to do to move forward.

Evening Journal

Today I am grateful for:

____

Did I make decisions in alignment with my best self? Where could I improve?

____

____

____

____

____

Was I kind towards the people around me? Where could I have been more considerate?

____

____

____

____

____

What temptations did I resist? What vices did I fight?

____

____

____

____

____

What was the biggest lesson I learned today?

What can I do better tomorrow?

Any other thoughts:

DAY FORTY-THREE DATE:

____

Morning Journal

There is a river of creation, and time is a violent stream. As soon as one thing comes into sight, it is swept past and another is carried down: it too will be taken on its way.

My word for today is:

____

My top five things to achieve today are:

____

____

____

____

____

Practical Exercise: Stay in the moment, for this too will pass

Get yourself in the flow to truly experience the current moment as it happens. Choose a task that you enjoy, something challenging but not too difficult, such as going for a run, doing some colouring, doing a puzzle, etc. As you are performing your activity, break it down into little parts, like running to the next lamppost, colouring with a particular shade, solving a particular section of the puzzle. Appreciate what you're doing right now while anticipating what is going to happen next and enjoy going with the flow.

Evening Journal

Today I am grateful for:

___

Did I make decisions in alignment with my best self? Where could I improve?

___
___
___
___
___

Was I kind towards the people around me? Where could I have been more considerate?

___
___
___
___
___

What temptations did I resist? What vices did I fight?

___
___
___
___
___

What was the biggest lesson I learned today?

What can I do better tomorrow?

Any other thoughts:

DAY FORTY-FOUR DATE:

____

Morning Journal

All things are in a process of change. You yourself are subject to constant alteration and gradual decay. So too is the whole universe.

My word for today is:

____

My top five things to achieve today are:

____

____

____

____

____

Practical Exercise: Memento Mori – Meditation on death

Now is a good time to do the meditation on death again.

Sit down and make yourself comfortable, ensuring your back is supported.

Take a moment to focus on your breath. Observe it as you inhale and exhale… Inhale and exhale…

And as you inhale, feel that breath filling you with warming energy, helping you relax.

And as you exhale, breathe out any negativity, any stress, any worry.

Continue to inhale that warming energy and exhale any negativity.

Now as you inhale feel yourself sinking down…down…down… Going deep into the earth.

You feel perfectly safe. Nothing can harm you here.

You find yourself standing on the edge of a river. Ahead of you is a small boat, a tall, silent figure dressed in black waiting patiently in the boat for you.

He holds out a hand and beckons you to join him on board.

You realise this is the River Styx, the ferryman, come to take you to the afterlife.

Once you cross this river, you will never be able to return. This is the end of your journey. Once you cross this river, you will be at peace, free from fear and pain.

But once you cross this river, you will never be able to see those you love again.

You imagine how everyone you know will feel when they learn about your passing. What will they say about you? Will they say you lived a good life? Will they say you always tried to do your best?

You think about the decisions you made that you regret. How did you learn from those experiences? How did you use them to do better in the future?

Now you think about the moments when you were at your happiest and felt content. What were you doing? How could you have brought more happiness into your life?

The ferryman beckons to you again, but you shake your head. Now is not your time to travel with him.

He nods, knowing you will return to this place again.

You feel yourself travelling back to your body. Take a moment to appreciate the simple fact you are alive at this time, with a future of possibility ahead of you.

Notice your breath again, feeling gratitude for your life as you inhale and exhale.

And when you are ready, open your eyes.

Journal your experiences.

Evening Journal

Today I am grateful for:

___

Did I make decisions in alignment with my best self? Where could I improve?

___

___

___

___

___

Was I kind towards the people around me? Where could I have been more considerate?

___

___

___

___

___

What temptations did I resist? What vices did I fight?

___

___

___

___

___

What was the biggest lesson I learned today?

What can I do better tomorrow?

Any other thoughts:

DAY FORTY-FIVE DATE:

Morning Journal

The termination of an activity, the pause when an impulse or judgement is finished – this is a sort of death, but no harm in it… So too there is nothing to fear in the termination, the pause, and the change of your whole life.

My word for today is:

My top five things to achieve today are:

Practical Exercise – Prepare for the worst

Pick an event you have coming up and list everything that could possibly go wrong or even stop it from happening altogether. Include anything you can think of, no matter how unlikely. For example, nobody could have predicted the pandemic of 2020, but that didn't prevent it from happening, meaning many people had to cancel weddings, holidays, celebrations, etc. As long as something *might* happen, include it on your list. The point of this exercise is to prepare yourself for *every* eventuality.

____

____

____

____

____

____

____

____

____

____

____

____

____

Once you've completed your list, go back and imagine how it would make you feel if each of the items actually happened. Really immerse yourself in that feeling, as if you're experiencing it right now, so should that event occur, you already know how you'd deal with it.

Finally, for each item, note what you could do to either minimise the likelihood of it occurring or, if it's outside of your control (as most things are), what you can do to minimise its impact. Now if the worst really does happen, you'll be better equipped to deal with it on every level.

Evening Journal

Today I am grateful for:

____

Did I make decisions in alignment with my best self? Where could I improve?

____

____

____

____

____

Was I kind towards the people around me? Where could I have been more considerate?

____

____

____

____

____

What temptations did I resist? What vices did I fight?

____

____

____

____

____

What was the biggest lesson I learned today?

What can I do better tomorrow?

Any other thoughts:

DAY FORTY-SIX DATE:

Morning Journal

I do my own duty: the other things do not distract me.

My word for today is:

My top five things to achieve today are:

Practical Exercise - Focus on what you can control with goal setting

It's time to check in on the goals you set for yourself on day 6. How are you doing? Are you meeting your targets or are you slipping?

Evening Journal

Today I am grateful for:

____

Did I make decisions in alignment with my best self? Where could I improve?

____

____

____

____

____

Was I kind towards the people around me? Where could I have been more considerate?

____

____

____

____

____

What temptations did I resist? What vices did I fight?

____

____

____

____

____

What was the biggest lesson I learned today?

____

____

____

____

____

What can I do better tomorrow?

____

____

____

____

____

Any other thoughts:

____

____

____

____

____

DAY FORTY-SEVEN DATE:

Morning Journal

All that happens is an event either within your natural ability to bear it, or not. So if it is an event within that ability, do not complain, but bear it as you were born to. If outside that ability, do not complain either; it will take you away before you have the chance for complaint. Remember, though, that you are by nature born to bear all that your own judgement can decide bearable, or tolerate in action, if you represent it to yourself as benefit or duty.

My word for today is:

____

My top five things to achieve today are:

____

____

____

____

____

Practical Exercise – Training your mind to accept your fate

It's time to return to the exercise you first did on day 17.

Make a commitment that you will not complain about anything today, no matter what. For example, if you get delayed on your way to work, that's okay. Tomorrow you'll leave earlier.

Make a note of how many times you forget and let yourself complain about something. Have you complained less than the last time you did this exercise?

Evening Journal

Today I am grateful for:

___

Did I make decisions in alignment with my best self? Where could I improve?

___

___

___

___

___

Was I kind towards the people around me? Where could I have been more considerate?

___

___

___

___

___

What temptations did I resist? What vices did I fight?

___

___

___

___

___

What was the biggest lesson I learned today?

____

____

____

____

____

What can I do better tomorrow?

____

____

____

____

____

Any other thoughts:

____

____

____

____

____

DAY FORTY-EIGHT DATE:

____

Morning Journal

All things are the same: familiar in experience, transient in time, sordid in substance. Everything now is as it was in the days of those we have buried.

My word for today is:

____

My top five things to achieve today are:

____

____

____

____

____

Practical Exercise - Stoic reflection

Choose a Stoic quote that speaks to you and write your thoughts on what it means and how you can incorporate it into your practises. Do you think this will be easy or difficult for you? What challenges can you anticipate and how can you overcome them?

Evening Journal

Today I am grateful for:

____

Did I make decisions in alignment with my best self? Where could I improve?

____

____

____

____

____

Was I kind towards the people around me? Where could I have been more considerate?

____

____

____

____

____

What temptations did I resist? What vices did I fight?

____

____

____

____

____

What was the biggest lesson I learned today?

____

____

____

____

____

What can I do better tomorrow?

____

____

____

____

____

Any other thoughts:

____

____

____

____

____

DAY FORTY-NINE DATE:

____

Morning Journal

You should leave another's wrong where it lies.

My word for today is:

____

My top five things to achieve today are:

____

____

____

____

____

Practical Exercise - Be your best self

Think about an argument or disagreement you've recently been involved in. Journal your motives and actions. Try and be as objective as possible, as if you were discussing someone else. What did you do wrong? What could you have done differently? Why do you think you behaved in the way you did? What other explanations might there be for your behaviour? How would a Stoic approach have looked?

Next, look at the motives and actions of the other person. What are the possible explanations for why they did what they did? What might be a factor for them that you are unaware of? What might be going on in their life that impacted their reactions to you?

When you are finished, choose the kindest explanation you can come with for the other party's behaviour and the harshest explanation for your own.

Write them out here:

____

____

____

____

____

____

____

____

____

____

____

____

____

How does this change your understanding of the situation? What will you do differently when something similar occurs in the future?

In the future I will:

____

____

____

____

____

Evening Journal

Today I am grateful for:

____

Did I make decisions in alignment with my best self? Where could I improve?

____

____

____

____

____

Was I kind towards the people around me? Where could I have been more considerate?

____

____

____

____

____

What temptations did I resist? What vices did I fight?

____

____

____

____

____

What was the biggest lesson I learned today?

What can I do better tomorrow?

Any other thoughts:

DAY FIFTY DATE:

Morning Journal

If he is going wrong, teach him kindly and show him what he has failed to see. If you can't do that, blame yourself – or perhaps not even yourself.

My word for today is:

My top five things to achieve today are:

Practical Exercise - Loving kindness meditation

Make yourself comfortable with your back supported and close your eyes. Turn your attention to your breath and observe as you inhale and exhale...inhale and exhale...

And as you breathe, feel yourself filling with peace and perfect love. With every exhalation, breathe out your stress, fear, and worry, and with every inhalation draw in more peace and love until you feel a deep, fulfilling calmness. Know that the universe loves you. You are worthy of love. You deserve peace and love at all times.

As you feel this beautiful sensation of calm and peace, think of someone you love, your partner, your children, your parents, a close friend. Whoever you think about, send that beautiful peace in their direction. See them being filled with love and harmony until they are as calm and happy as you are in this moment.

Do this again for all your close loved ones.

Now move on to people to whom you are not so close. Perhaps your colleagues, your neighbours, the person who regularly serves you at your favourite restaurant. Send this love and peace towards them, filling them up with calm, peace, and contentment.

Finally, think about those who have done you wrong, those you do not like, those who have made your life difficult. They, too, deserve love, so send them the same waves of love and peace, accepting them for who they are and knowing that they are worthy of love because they have taught you valuable lessons and helped you become the person you are today.

When you have finished sending love to everyone who needs it, sit a little longer, feeling this beautiful, peaceful energy.

When you are ready, open your eyes, knowing that this love and peace is always with you.

Journal your experiences.

Evening Journal

Today I am grateful for:

____

Did I make decisions in alignment with my best self? Where could I improve?

____

____

____

____

____

Was I kind towards the people around me? Where could I have been more considerate?

____

____

____

____

____

What temptations did I resist? What vices did I fight?

____

____

____

____

____

What was the biggest lesson I learned today?

____
____
____
____
____

What can I do better tomorrow?

____
____
____
____
____

Any other thoughts:

____
____
____
____
____

DAY FIFTY-ONE DATE:

____

Morning Journal

Either you live on here, used to it now; or you retire, your own decision to leave; or you die, your service done. No other choice. Be cheerful, then.

My word for today is:

____

My top five things to achieve today are:

____

____

____

____

____

Daily Exercise: Practice misfortune

Following on from the exercise where you restricted your diet for a short period, you can take this a step further by abstaining from food completely for 24 hours. As long as you drink plenty of water, an occasional day without food will not do you any harm (although check with your doctor if you have any medical concerns).

Evening Journal

Today I am grateful for:

____

Did I make decisions in alignment with my best self? Where could I improve?

____

____

____

____

____

Was I kind towards the people around me? Where could I have been more considerate?

____

____

____

____

____

What temptations did I resist? What vices did I fight?

____

____

____

____

____

What was the biggest lesson I learned today?

____

What can I do better tomorrow?

Any other thoughts:

DAY FIFTY-TWO DATE:

____

Morning Journal

No more roundabout discussion of what makes a good man. Be one!

My word for today is:

____

My top five things to achieve today are:

____

____

____

____

____

Daily exercise: Turn the obstacle upside down

Look back at the exercise you did on day 22. Have you made any progress towards your goal or are obstacles still getting in your way? Make a list of everything which is stopping you from progressing.

Now list all the actions you can take to turn these obstacles and use them to your advantage.

What is the next step you need to take towards your goal? Make a commitment to yourself that you will do it today.

Evening Journal

Today I am grateful for:

____

Did I make decisions in alignment with my best self? Where could I improve?

____

____

____

____

____

Was I kind towards the people around me? Where could I have been more considerate?

____

____

____

____

____

What temptations did I resist? What vices did I fight?

____

____

____

____

____

What was the biggest lesson I learned today?

What can I do better tomorrow?

Any other thoughts:

DAY FIFTY-THREE DATE:

Morning Journal

Keep constantly in your mind an impression of the whole of time and the whole of existence – and the thought that each individual thing is, on the scale of existence, a mere fig-seed; on the scale of time, one turn of a drill.

My word for today is:

My top five things to achieve today are:

Practical Exercise: Stay in the moment, for this too will pass

Decide that you are going to find six new things about your environment today. Actively look for things you haven't noticed before or pay attention to how things have subtly changed since yesterday. Not only will this help you be more mindful, it also demonstrates very obviously how nothing ever stays the same.

Evening Journal

Today I am grateful for:

____

Did I make decisions in alignmDid I make decisions in alignment with my best self? Where could I improve?

____

____

____

____

____

Was I kind towards the people around me? Where could I have been more considerate?

____

____

____

____

____

What temptations did I resist? What vices did I fight?

____

____

____

____

____

What was the biggest lesson I learned today?

____

____

____

____

____

What can I do better tomorrow?

____

____

____

____

____

Any other thoughts:

____

____

____

____

____

DAY FIFTY-FOUR DATE:

____

Morning Journal

It is the nature of all things to change, to perish and be transformed, so that in succession different things can come to be.

My word for today is:

____

My top five things to achieve today are:

____

____

____

____

____

Practical Exercise – Memento Mori. Revisit your eulogy

It's worth regularly updating your eulogy. This will help you be aware of the progress you're making on your Stoic journey, as well as highlighting what more you can do to be a better person.

Look back on the eulogy you wrote on day 24. How would you change it? What new positive things can you say about yourself? What changes have you noticed in your behaviour?

Evening Journal

Today I am grateful for:

Did I make decisions in alignment with my best self? Where could I improve?

Was I kind towards the people around me? Where could I have been more considerate?

What temptations did I resist? What vices did I fight?

What was the biggest lesson I learned today?

What can I do better tomorrow?

Any other thoughts:

DAY FIFTY-FIVE DATE:

____

Morning Journal

Many grains of incense on the same altar. One falls to ash first, another later: no difference.

My word for today is:

____

My top five things to achieve today are:

____

____

____

____

____

Practical Exercise – Prepare for the worst with visualization

This can be a very emotional exercise, so when you do it, choose a time and place where you won't be disturbed so you can fully immerse yourself in the moment without feeling like you have to self-censor for the sake of those around you.

Choose one of the worst things you could imagine happening to you. It might be losing a loved one; it could be experiencing a life-changing accident; perhaps you want to think about becoming homeless following a redundancy. Pick something that is your absolute worst nightmare, the one thing you really *don't* want to see come true.

Sit yourself comfortably, making sure your back is supported, so you can meditate without being distracted by your body needing to fidget. Close your eyes and imagine someone telling you the news you didn't want to hear. Picture their face, the sadness in their eyes as they tell you what happened and how sorry they are for you. Allow yourself to be flooded with emotion as you feel denial it could be possible, anger that it's happened, sadness that things will never be the same again. If you need to cry, cry.

Don't think about what to do next. This is not the time to come up with contingency plans. Instead, immerse yourself completely in the feelings of the moment. Know that there was absolutely nothing you could have done to change this outcome, so all you can do is accept that this is how it is and adjust your reality accordingly.

This too will pass. No matter how badly you feel in the moment, this moment is not forever.

Evening Journal

Today I am grateful for:

____

Did I make decisions in alignment with my best self? Where could I improve?

____

____

____

____

____

Was I kind towards the people around me? Where could I have been more considerate?

____

____

____

____

____

What temptations did I resist? What vices did I fight?

____

____

____

____

____

What was the biggest lesson I learned today?

What can I do better tomorrow?

Any other thoughts:

DAY FIFTY-SIX DATE:

Morning Journal

You deserve what you're going through. You would rather become good tomorrow than be good today.

My word for today is:

____

My top five things to achieve today are:

____

____

____

____

____

Practical Exercise – Focus on what you can control with goal setting

It's time to check in on the goals you set for yourself on day 6. How are you doing? Are you meeting your targets or are you slipping? What can you do to get yourself back on track?

Evening Journal

Today I am grateful for:

____

Did I make decisions in alignment with my best self? Where could I improve?

____

____

____

____

____

Was I kind towards the people around me? Where could I have been more considerate?

____

____

____

____

____

What temptations did I resist? What vices did I fight?

____

____

____

____

____

What was the biggest lesson I learned today?

____

____

____

____

____

What can I do better tomorrow?

____

____

____

____

____

Any other thoughts:

____

____

____

____

____

DAY FIFTY-SEVEN DATE:

____

Morning Journal

Do not be ashamed of help. It is your task to achieve your assigned duty, like a soldier in a scaling party. What, then, if you are lame and cannot climb the parapet by yourself, but this is made possible by another's help?

My word for today is:

____

My top five things to achieve today are:

____

____

____

____

____

Practical Exercise: Prepare for the worst by talking to your future self

It is time to check in with your future self.

Make a commitment that if anything negative happens to you today, before you react you will take a moment to ask yourself: "How will I be feeling about this event in ten years' time?"

If you still find yourself upset, imagine yourself sitting down with yourself ten years into the future. What advice would they give you? Would you be telling yourself not to worry, that everything's going to be all right, it'll all work out in the end?

Journal your experiences.

Evening Journal

Today I am grateful for:

____

Did I make decisions in alignment with my best self? Where could I improve?

____

____

____

____

____

Was I kind towards the people around me? Where could I have been more considerate?

____

____

____

____

____

What temptations did I resist? What vices did I fight?

____

____

____

____

____

What was the biggest lesson I learned today?

____

____

____

____

____

What can I do better tomorrow?

____

____

____

____

____

Any other thoughts:

____

____

____

____

____

DAY FIFTY-EIGHT DATE:

____

Morning Journal

Remember that to change course or accept correction leaves you just as free as you were. The action is your own, driven by your own impulse and judgement, indeed your own intelligence.

My word for today is:

____

My top five things to achieve today are:

____

____

____

____

____

Practical Exercise - Stoic reflection

Choose a Stoic quote that speaks to you and write your thoughts on what it means and how you can incorporate it into your practises. Do you think this will be easy or difficult for you? What challenges can you anticipate and how can you overcome them?

Evening Journal

Today I am grateful for:

Did I make decisions in alignment with my best self? Where could I improve?

Was I kind towards the people around me? Where could I have been more considerate?

What temptations did I resist? What vices did I fight?

What was the biggest lesson I learned today?

What can I do better tomorrow?

Any other thoughts:

DAY FIFTY-NINE DATE:

____

Morning Journal

As soon as you wake from sleep, ask yourself: 'Will it make any difference to me if others criticize what is in fact just and true?' No, it will not.

My word for today is:

____

My top five things to achieve today are:

____

____

____

____

____

Practical Exercise – Be your best self

Make a list of all your weaknesses, bad habits and things you would like to change about yourself.

Choose one and come up with a way in which you can do the opposite to replace your negative tendencies with a more positive action. For example, maybe you love getting that first coffee from Starbucks. Get a reusable cup and make your own or even switch to juice instead of coffee. Ask yourself: what would my best self do?

In the future, I will:

Evening Journal

Today I am grateful for:

____

Did I make decisions in alignment with my best self? Where could I improve?

____

____

____

____

____

Was I kind towards the people around me? Where could I have been more considerate?

____

____

____

____

____

What temptations did I resist? What vices did I fight?

____

____

____

____

____

What was the biggest lesson I learned today?

____

____

____

____

____

What can I do better tomorrow?

____

____

____

____

____

Any other thoughts:

____

____

____

____

____

DAY SIXTY DATE:

Morning Journal

What universal nature brings to each is brought to his benefit. The benefit stands at the time of its bringing.

My word for today is:

My top five things to achieve today are:

Practical Exercise – Loving kindness meditation

Make yourself comfortable with your back supported and close your eyes. Turn your attention to your breath and observe as you inhale and exhale…inhale and exhale…

And as you breathe, feel yourself filling with peace and perfect love. With every exhalation, breathe out your stress, fear, and worry, and with every inhalation draw in more peace and love until you feel a deep, fulfilling calmness. Know that the universe loves you. You are worthy of love. You deserve peace and love at all times.

As you feel this beautiful sensation of calm and peace, think of someone you love, your partner, your children, your parents, a close friend. Whoever you think about, send that beautiful peace in their direction. See them being filled with love and harmony until they are as calm and happy as you are in this moment.

Do this again for all your close loved ones.

Now move on to people to whom you are not so close. Perhaps your colleagues, your neighbours, the person who regularly serves you at your favourite restaurant. Send this love and peace towards them, filling them up with calm, peace, and contentment.

Finally, think about those who have done you wrong, those you do not like, those who have made your life difficult. They, too, deserve love, so send them the same waves of love and peace, accepting them for who they are and knowing that they are worthy of love because they have taught you valuable lessons and helped you become the person you are today.

When you have finished sending love to everyone who needs it, sit a little longer, feeling this beautiful, peaceful energy.

When you are ready, open your eyes, knowing that this love and peace is always with you.

Evening Journal

Today I am grateful for:

____

Did I make decisions in alignment with my best self? Where could I improve?

____

____

____

____

____

Was I kind towards the people around me? Where could I have been more considerate?

____

____

____

____

____

What temptations did I resist? What vices did I fight?

____

____

____

____

____

What was the biggest lesson I learned today?

What can I do better tomorrow?

Any other thoughts:

THANKS FOR READING

I hope that you enjoyed reading this journal and that the practical exercises have been valuable.

I love hearing your opinions and feedback and would appreciate you taking the time to leave an Amazon review – I will do my best to reply to all questions asked!

Be sure to check out my email list, where I am constantly adding tons of value. You will also receive my three-page cheat sheet that you can use for reference as you move forward on your stoic path.

You can sign up here: bouchardpublishing.com/stoicism.

Kindest Regards,
Jason Hemlock

Made in United States
Troutdale, OR
12/21/2023

16279866R00156